Building A
Man-to-Man
Defense

Bob Huggins

ISBN: 978-1-58518-172-8
Library of Congress Control Number: 99-69030
Cover design: Jeanne Hamilton
Text design: Jeanne Hamilton
Front cover photo: Jim McIsaac/Getty Images

Coaches Choice
P.O. Box 1828
Monterey, CA 93942
www.coacheschoice.com

Contents

Introduction

The intention of this book is to show you how to build a man-to-man defense for your team. I will attempt to show you the way we teach the players in our program using the whole-part-whole method of learning. Initially, I will explain the overall picture, purpose and philosophy of the defense and then break it down piece by piece. The breakdown will begin with one-on-one drills and build back to the five-on-five concepts we have developed for our team defense.

Over the last 20 years, many dramatic changes in this game have occurred. For example, the athleticism of the individual players is far superior to any other time in basketball history. Rule changes have also affected our style of play and how we defend both on the ball and away from the ball. Examples of rule changes that have influenced our staff to reevaluate our coverages include (1) the shot clock, (2) the three-point shot and (3) the five-second closely guarded rule. Hopefully, some of the ideas, techniques and terms that are detailed in this book will be as beneficial to you and your athletes as they have been to our teams.

Diagram Key

COACH = **C**

OFFENSIVE PLAYER = ◯

SPECIFIC OFFENSIVE PLAYERS = ① ② ③ ④ ⑤

OFFENSIVE PLAYER WITH THE BALL = ◯

DEFENSIVE PLAYER = X

SPECIFIC DEFENSIVE PLAYERS = X_1 X_2 X_3 X_4 X_5

PASS = - - - →

CUT OR PATH OF THE PLAYER = ⟶

DRIBBLER = ∿∿∿

SCREEN = ⟶|

OFFENSIVE PLAYER O4 WHO STARTS WITH THE BALL, PASSES IT TO
O2 AND THEN SCREENS FOR O3, WHO USES HIS SCREEN TO CUT

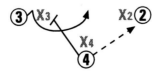

1

Philosophy of the Defensive Box Theory

A few years ago, our practice time was reduced, and we became very concerned that we would not have enough time to teach everything that we normally do during the season. We examined all of our practice schedules from previous years and evaluated the necessity of everything we were teaching. We questioned all the techniques we had been using to see if they had value within our overall philosophy of how we wanted to play the game.

For example, my father has run a very successful summer camp for years. I always laughed to myself when a guest lecturer would come in and teach the two-hand chest pass as a fundamental for today's game. The fact is that pressure defenses have all but eliminated the two-hand chest pass the same way they have made the two-hand set shot obsolete. In the evaluation of our techniques, one of the questions we posed about our defense was why we still denied the wing pass. The only rationale I could come up with was that I had always been coached to deny the wing, so it must be worthwhile.

When I began playing basketball, the dominant philosophy was to force the ball into the middle of the court, where all the help was. We protected the key area with all our help-side defenders keeping the bigger players home and trying to funnel everything to them. With this concept of defense, it makes perfect sense to keep the ball out of the side of the floor; thus, denying the wing was fundamentally sound.

In our defensive philosophy of forcing the ball to be passed or dribbled to the side of the floor, why would we deny the ball from going where we wanted it to be directed in the first place? Therefore, we changed this technique to fit our overall defensive philosophy—no longer denying any pass to the wing or the corner, but rather, simply requiring that the defender make the offensive player catch the ball while he is going away from the basket.

When you are looking at your own defensive techniques, think about all of your help-side theories and how they relate to your overall defensive philosophy. Changing this one concept seemed to crystallize an idea we have had for a long time and haven't been teaching very well. The following pages will define the terms we use to describe the box theory.

2

Terminology

TERM—*BOX THEORY*

Our man-to-man defense is based on the *Box Theory*. The court is divided into two boxes: the ball-side box and the help- side box (Diagram 1).

Diagram 1

    We attempt to force the ball into one side of the floor, which then becomes the ball-side box, and then keep it there. We will not deny any passes that take the ball deeper into the box. In fact, we encourage this type of pass, as long as the offensive player receiving the ball catches it moving away from the basket (Diagram 2).

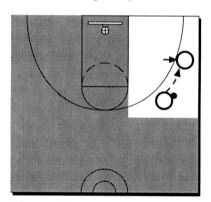

Diagram 2

Once we have the ball in a box, we deny every pass that would make the box larger (Diagram 3).

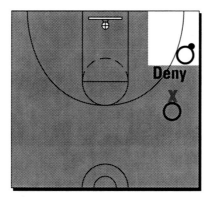

Diagram 3

Any pass that would make our defense change boxes (sides of the floor) is denied even harder (Diagram 4).

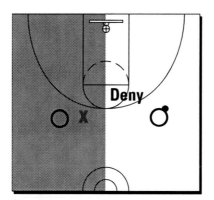

Diagram 4

All of our defensive denial drills now revolve around keeping the ball in the box and keeping the box as small as possible. We still work hard on denial drills—not just on denying the pass to the wing which shortens the box.

Forcing the ball to be passed or dribbled further into the box decreases the area that we have to defend as a team. We believe that if you are able to guard the man with the ball with three defenders, it is almost certain that we can stop him. By decreasing the amount of space we have to cover, it is easier for our defenders to be able to accomplish this goal. All of our defenders must be close enough to take one big step and have a foot in the box (Diagram 5).

Diagram 5

The deeper the ball is penetrated, the smaller the box becomes and the closer the defenders can get to the player with the ball (Diagram 6).

Diagram 6

TERM—*ON THE LINE, UP THE LINE*

On the line, up the line is the term we use for the position of the defensive players who are not guarding the person with the ball. All players "off the ball" should draw a direct line between their man and the ball and then position themselves on that line. This maneuver accomplishes the following things:

*   It takes away the vision from the offensive player. Anytime you can take away the vision of an offensive player, you are increasing the defenders' chances of being successful.

*   It discourages the skip pass by making the receiver more difficult to see and the pass easier to intercept. A completed skip pass makes the defense change boxes from one side of the floor to the other.

*   If you decide to add trapping into your defensive scheme, it will make it much easier to trap in either a half-court or full-court matchup.

Below are two examples of defensive players being on the line, up the line (Diagram 7 and 8).

Diagram 7

Diagram 8

The on-the-line, up-the-line theory is in contrast to the concept of the off-the-ball defender being in a "flat triangle" position. The flat triangle position is taught by many coaches, and in fact, we used this technique for years. It means that you place the defender one big step off the direct line toward the basket.

Below are examples of off-the-ball defenders being in a "flat triangle" (Diagrams 9 and 10).

Diagram 9

Diagram 10

As you can see by comparing the diagrams, these defenders are closer to the basket than they would be if they were on the line, up the line. The triangle is formed by one point being the player with the ball, another point being the man being guarded and the third point being the defender one step off the direct line. This is a sound defensive concept, but we do not feel that the defender can do as many things from this position as he can from being directly on the line.

The biggest reason that coaches give for teaching the flat triangle position is that the defender will not have to turn his head to see both the ball and the man he is checking. I believe that this is only true if neither the ball nor the player is moving. But in reality, both the ball and the person are constantly in motion; therefore, the defender ends up turning his head, anyway, and may as well be in the more aggressive position of on the line, up the line.

TERM—*SPRINT TO HELP*

The term *sprint to help* is used when a defender goes from checking the ball to being in a help position on the line, up the line. We found that the natural tendency of a defender at this moment is to drop more toward the basket than toward the ball; therefore, we had to devise drills that taught our players to react by immediately sprinting to an on-the-line, up-the-line position.

The diagram below is a description of the responsibility the defender has when his player passes the ball (Diagram 11).

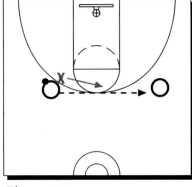

Diagram 11

- The defender is guarding the ball on the wing.

- The ball is skipped to the opposite wing. While the ball is in the air, the defender must sprint to the middle of the floor so he can be close enough to be within one step of having a foot in the box.

- The defender positions himself to be off his man and in a direct line between the ball and his man—on the line, up the line.

TERM—*PISTOL POSITION*

Another requirement for the off-the-ball defender is to be in pistol position. When a defender is in an on-the-line, up-the-line position, he gets into an "open stance." This stance means that both of the defenders' toes are on the imaginary line between the ball and the man he is defending.

The defender in an open stance needs to be in an athletic position with his knees bent, his hips down his back straight, as if he were sitting on a stool. This is the same "ready position" used by infielders in baseball and linebackers in football. Being flexed at the knees and hips allows the athlete to be quicker in his initial movement.

The term *pistols* comes from the position of the hands by the players in an open stance off the ball. The off-the-ball defender points at the ball with the index finger of his hand closest to the ball, and points toward his man with the other index finger. It should appear that this player is pointing a six-shooter at both the ball and his man.

Correct pistol position:

- Allows the defender to keep track of both the ball and his man.

- Helps the coaches quickly observe players who are properly aligned and those who are out of position.

- If the defender has his hands up and is not pointing toward the ball and the man, he has lost track of one or the other.

- The arms should be away from the body at about a 140-degree angle so that the defender can meet and shed screens. We tell our players to keep their arms in this position so that the potential screeners cannot get contact on their body.

- The defender's head must be constantly turning to see not only his man and the ball, but also any offensive players approaching who could potentially set a screen on him.

- The pistol position helps the off-the-ball defenders see where everyone on the floor is positioned so they can make straight-line rotations in a help situation.

- The defender rotates by taking a drop step in a straight line to the man we are rotating toward, which requires good vision of the floor.

3

One-on-One Defensive Drills

Defensive basketball is not easy. It consists of hard work, intelligence, courage and aggressiveness all wrapped into one. It is no secret that these are the same characteristics of every successful athlete, regardless of his sport. Some coaches believe that an athlete either has these traits or he doesn't, but I have seen young men develop in these areas consistently throughout a season's work in a defensive-oriented program. Personally, we feel that these traits can be developed if the athlete truly desires to be a successful player. Mental toughness is a benefit derived from defensive work. Seldom can it be obtained during the offensive drills.

The defensive player is under constant pressure to neutralize his opponent's best effort. Therefore, constant pressure needs to be applied to him in defensive practice situations. As a result of this kind of practice atmosphere, players will become better performers under pressure.

Team discipline is not a problem on the defensive-minded team because the players are accustomed to sacrificing their personal goals and comforts for the good of the group. These players will truly develop the attitude of wanting to do whatever is necessary to win for the team. These types of athletes arrive early and stay late to improve their own game or to help a teammate. They are not easily discouraged by mistakes and can quickly recover, because they know that whatever happened can be overcome by the effort of the team. These athletes hold themselves accountable for errors that are made and accept the correction that comes from the coaching staff.

We want this type of team, and the only way to have it is through hard, demanding, relentless practice. We expect everyone to be striving to improve on a daily basis. The development of an outstanding defensive team requires hard work by both players and coaches. As coaches, we must be willing to work longer, harder and smarter than anyone we compete against. The results are well worth the time and effort spent.

The following drills are the ones we have selected to teach our players the skills they need to master in order to defend another individual player. It is essential that drills carry over into instinctive habits that the athletes can use at game speed. Some of these drills are done with a mass group, some are done one-on-one spread out around the court and some are done in small groups split up by position.

STANCE

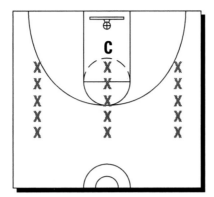

Diagram 12

- Feet are approximately shoulder-width apart with one foot slightly ahead of the other.

- Athletic position with knees bent, hips down, back straight and head up, as if the player were sitting on a stool.

- Carry your hands with one hand above the ear and the other slightly below the ear on that side.

WALL STANCE

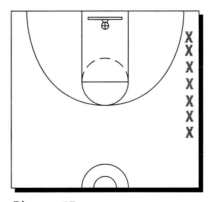

Diagram 13

- Same principles of body positioning as the drill above, except with their backs against the wall.

- This is a great drill to develop leg strength and mental toughness.

STEP-SLIDE

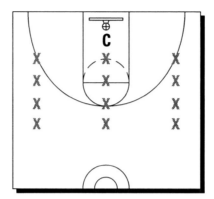

Diagram 14

- Players get into the stance as it has previously been described.

- When the coach points in a certain direction, they step in that direction with their lead foot and slide their trail foot. Their trail foot should never leave the floor.

- Their feet should not come together, but rather stay about shoulder-width apart or wider.

- The hand on the side of the ball should remain up to discourage a direct pass, while they should keep their other hand low, using it as a "drag hand" to prevent a crossover dribble.

SWING STEP

- Use the same formation as the Step-Slide Drill.

- The players get into their stance as previously described, all with the same foot forward.

- On command, they swing the forward foot in the direction the coach points and step-slide.

- The swing should be a quarter turn—not a half turn in order to allow the defenders to keep the offense in front of them and not completely "open the gate" to the basket.

- The feet do not come together, and should stay about shoulder-width apart.

- The hands have the same positioning as they did in the Step-Slide Drill.

WAVE

- The players line up in the same formation used for the Step-Slide and the Swing Step drills.

- This drill combines the Stance Drill, the Step-Slide Drill and the Swing Step Drill.

- Players move on the command and point of the coach.
- We can also include loose ball and charge drills into this section, with the players diving for an imaginary ball or taking an imaginary charge on command.

ADVANCE-RETREAT

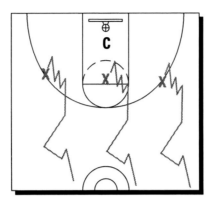

Diagram 15

- Players get into a proper defensive stance.
- Players step-slide, advancing and retreating on command while keeping their feet wide.
- When advancing, they should lead with their front foot. When retreating, their back foot leads.
- They slide to half court, changing direction in quarter turns on the coach's command.
- The hands of the players should remain up, in an active position.

MIRROR

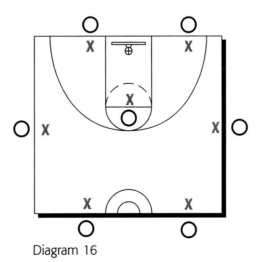

Diagram 16

- Players pair up with another player of about equal quickness and stand on each side of any line in the gym, giving themselves lots of room.

- The player designated as offense attempts to shake the defender by running up and down the line, changing directions as quickly as possible.

- The job of the defender is to step-slide up and down the line mirroring the offense and keep his nose to the offensive player's navel.

- This drill can last as long as the coach desires.

ZIG ZAG

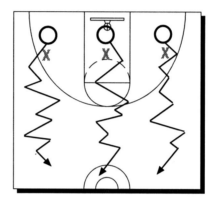

Diagram 17

- The offensive player dribbles down the floor (as shown in the diagram), while the defender step-slides and keeps his nose on the ball while making the offensive player turn.

- If the dribbler turns his back, the defender takes one retreat step straight back off the ball, not jumping from one side or the other.

READY-POINT-STICK

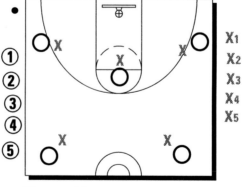

Diagram 18

- Players pair up with someone of equal quickness and spread out on the court.

- The defensive man gets into the stance described in the Stance Drill and yells, "Ready, ready, ready!"

- The offensive player takes a couple of dribbles in either direction. The defender attempts to force the dribbler to the sideline using the foot and hand techniques described earlier. The whole time the ball is being dribbled, the defender is yelling, "Point, point, point!"

- The offensive player then kills his dribble. When the ball is picked up, the defender yells, "Stick, stick, stick!" As he bellies up to the offensive player, the defender keeps his hands over his head, while keeping his knees bent and his butt down in a low stance. The defender does not stand up straight.

FORCE BASELINE AND CUT OFF

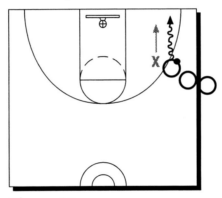

Diagram 19

- The defense forces the offense to go toward the baseline at an angle and then cuts the player off before he can turn the corner to the basket.

ONE-ON-ONE INFLUENCE TO THE SIDE OF THE FLOOR

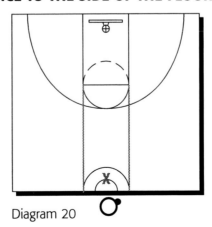

Diagram 20

- The offensive player begins with his back turned at half court

- The offensive player tries to drive by the defender while staying in the area the width of the lane, all the way to the baseline.

- The defender's job is to force the dribbler out of this area and toward the coach, who is standing on one of the sidelines.

DRIVING LINE

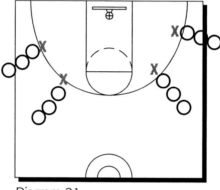

Diagram 21

- This drill can be run from anywhere on the offensive end of the court.

- The defender's goal is to play the offensive player one-on-one, attempting to force him to the baseline, create a turnover or rebound any missed shot.

- This drill can be run several ways. For example, the defender must stop one or any number of players determined by the coach before he goes to offense. The offense can also be limited to a specific direction or number of dribbles.

APPROACH

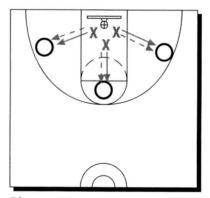

Diagram 22

- The defender starts about 15 feet from the offensive player and rolls the ball to him.

- He then sprints out to two thirds of the distance and then settles quickly into his stance and slides out to the player with the ball in a position to cut and influence the drive and also contest any potential shot.

- To begin with, have the offensive player not be live.

CLOSE OUT ON THE SHOOTER

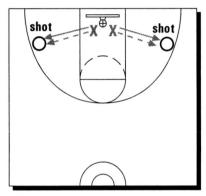

Diagram 23

- The defender starts under the basket and rolls the ball to the shooter on the wing or the high post.

- He sprints two thirds and then slides one third, trying to put pressure on the stationary shooter and then blocking out. This drill is live.

CLOSE OUT ON THE SHOOTER OR DRIVER

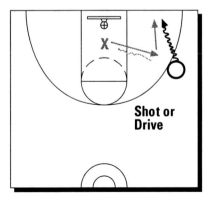

Diagram 24

- This drill is run the same way as shown in Diagram 23, except the offensive player has the freedom to drive if he thinks the defender has closed out off balance or too fast.

- The coach can limit the number of dribbles the offense can take, but at this point, the defender has to be able to defend both the shot and the drive with correct feet and hands; he still is responsible for blocking out to conclude the drill.

CLOSE OUT OFF THE SKIP PASS

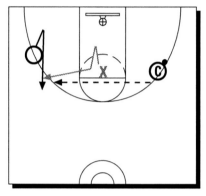

Diagram 25

- The defender starts in the key, using his hands as "pistols." The offensive player can move up or down the wing area, forcing the defender to constantly adjust to stay on the line and up the line.

- The coach then skips the ball to the offensive player, and the defender has to close out (two-thirds sprint and one-third sprint), influencing and containing any drive to the baseline and able to contest any shot.

CLOSE OUT OVER A SCREEN

Diagram 26

- The defender starts out in the "pistol" position in the middle of the key, checking an offensive player who is moving up and down on the help side of the floor. The defender must constantly adjust in order to stay on the line and up the line.

- A screener is also on the help side of the floor (You can have him use a football hand shield). As the coach skips the ball to the offensive player, the defender must use the correct closeout technique and also get over the screen at a good angle and slide out to put pressure on the shot and contain the drive.

- After the initial screen, the screener moves off the floor and out of the way of the one-on-one situation.

- As the defender is sprinting toward the offensive player, he must use his hands and feet to fight over the screen, trying not to let the offensive player get to his body.

- The screen cannot delay his progress to close out or make him run so far out of line to get around the screen that he does not have a good angle to close out to the ball.

- He fights quickly over the screen while in the sprint part of his closeout and then slides under control to a position that insures that the offensive player has to go baseline with the dribble.

VISION #1

Diagram 27

- This drill is intended to help the defender get on the line and up the line without losing vision of the ball or his man.

- The coach moves in possession of the basketball as the offensive player stays stationary.

- The defender must adjust to the movement of the coach and stay on line.

VISION #2

Diagram 28

- The defender uses the same fundamentals required in the Vision Drill, except that, in this drill, the offensive player moves while the coach with the ball is stationary.

- The offensive player can move up or down, closer or further from the coach with the ball.

VISION #3

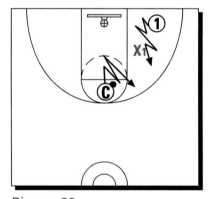

Diagram 29

- The defender again uses the same fundamentals of the foot and pistols position to stay on the line and up the line without losing vision of either the ball or his man.

- In this drill, both the coach and the offensive player are moving; therefore, it becomes more game-like for the defender.

SPRINT TO HELP

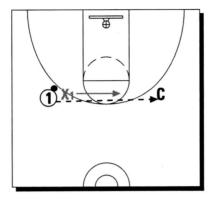

Diagram 30

- The defensive player is guarding the ball on the wing when the ball is skipped to the opposite wing.

- The defender must sprint to the middle of the floor while the ball is in the air and get to a position where he can be one big step away from having a foot in the new box.

- The defender must be both on the line and off the ball in the correct defensive position.

DENY THE FLASH CUT HIGH

Diagram 31

- The coach starts with the ball on the wing opposite the offensive player.

- When he slaps the ball or gives a verbal command, the offensive player makes a flash cut toward the basketball. He starts low and makes a small V cut preceding his direct path toward the ball.

- The defender starts in the pistol position on the line and up the line with vision of both the ball and his man.

- As the offensive player begins his V cut, the defender must adjust his position to stay in line.

- As the offensive cutter starts toward the ball, the defender must allow the cushion between them to gradually decrease as the offensive player cuts across the key.

- The defensive player gives some ground toward the ball for every step the offense player takes; at the same time, he allows the distance between them to slowly get smaller.

- He never lets the offensive player get to his body, using the pistol position with his hands to act as a buffer.

- The defender has been successful if the following holds true: (a) he never trails the cutter, (2) he beats him to the spot where he is trying to go, (3) he can make contact without fouling, and (4) he can keep the ball from being entered to the offensive player with a pass to the post area.

DENY THE FLASH CUT LOW

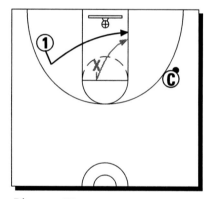

Diagram 32

- The coach has the ball on the opposite wing from the offensive player. The defender assumes the correct pistol position in the key.

- This time the offensive player begins his movement by V cutting high and then flashing hard low across the key toward the ball side of the court.

- The defender uses the same technique as in the previous drill, but this time he stops the low cut with the correct footwork and pistol position.

DENY THE FLASH AND RECOVER

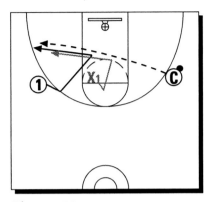

Diagram 33

- The coach starts with the ball on the wing, while the offensive player starts on the opposite side of the floor.

- The offense can start low and either flash high or start high and flash low to the ball side.

- If the defender stops the initial flash cut, the offensive player backs out to the help-side wing to receive a skip pass from the coach. The defender must then use the closeout principles and techniques discussed earlier.

JUMP TO THE BALL

Diagram 34

- This drill can and should be run on different parts of the half court.
- The offensive player starts with the ball while being defended.

- As the offensive player passes the ball to the coach, the defender checking the passer immediately adjusts his position by jumping in the direction of the pass while the ball is in the air.

- He gets into the on-the-line, up-the-line position.

DEFEND THE GIVE-AND-GO

Diagram 35

- This drill should be practiced in a variety of areas on the floor.

- The defender aggressively guards the offensive player with the ball.

- The offensive player passes the ball to the coach and cuts toward the basket.

- The defender jumps in the direction of the pass and forces the offensive player to go behind him. He puts his head on a swivel for vision and slides down the key with the cutter.

DEFEND THE GIVE-AND-GO IN EITHER DIRECTION

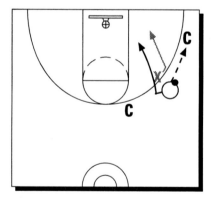

Diagram 36

- The defender has the same responsibilities and technique used in the previous drill, except this time the offensive player has a receiver on both sides of him and can pass in either direction.
- The defender must read the direction of the pass and adjust his position correctly.

DEFEND THE PASS AND GO AWAY

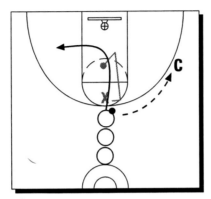

Diagram 37

- This drill should be run at different places on the court.
- After the offensive player passes the ball to the coach, he cuts to the basket and then goes to the help side of the floor.
- The defender jumps in the direction of the pass while the ball is in the air.
- As the cutter goes to the basket, he snaps his head without opening his stance and denies a return pass.
- As soon as the offensive player has cleared out to the help side, the defender assumes the pistol position in the key.

DEFEND THE PASS AND GO AWAY PLUS FLASH

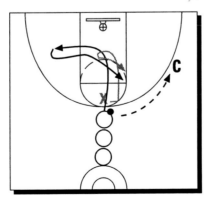

Diagram 38

- This drill utilizes the same technique and pattern as the previous drill, except that, at the end of the drill, it adds the maneuver of defending the flash.

- After the offensive player has passed, cut and cleared out to the help side of the court and the defender has assumed the pistol position in the key, the coach signals for the offensive man to flash toward the ball.

- By combining this drill with the previous drill, the defender has to carry over multiple defensive concepts.

DEFEND THE PASS AND GO AWAY PLUS CLOSE OUT

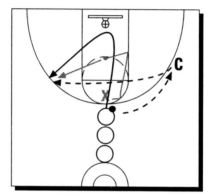

Diagram 39

- Same as the previous drills, as far as the pass and go away are concerned; but instead of flashing toward the ball, the coach skip passes the ball to the offensive player, and the defender must add correct closeout techniques to the end of the drill.

PUSH THE WING DRILL

Diagram 40

- Since we are attempting to have the offense bring the ball to the wing area, we will not deny the wing pass. We are only attempting to force the offensive player to catch the ball going away from the basket.

- As the offensive player begins his "pop out" cut to get open, the defender should have his arm and hand in the passing lane. He tries to avoid letting the offensive man get any contact with him by staying off in the direction of the ball.

DEFEND THE BACKDOOR CUT

Diagram 41

- The offensive player pops out to the perimeter, and at a predetermined place on the floor, he back cuts to the basket.

- The defender puts his head on a swivel and throws his back foot open and covers the back cut so that the only pass that can be thrown is the lob.

- As he closes down on the back cut, the defender throws his back arm out in the passing lane.

PUSH TO WING AND INFLUENCE

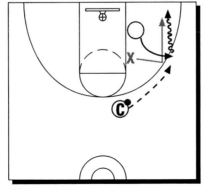

Diagram 42

- After the defender has forced the offensive man to catch the ball while moving from the basket—and the offensive player catches the ball—the defender must get off a step and influence the dribbler to the baseline and then cut him off before he can turn the corner.

POINT DENIAL

Diagram 43   Diagram 44

- Denying the ball to the point eliminates the simplest method that the offense can use to reverse the ball.

- The defender uses the same hand and arm in the passing lane technique as he did in the previous drill.

- The coach can add the backdoor cut from the point (Diagram 44) and defend it with the same technique as on the wing, swivel the head, open the back foot and throw the back arm in the passing lane, allowing only the lob pass.

DENIALS OUT OF THE BOX

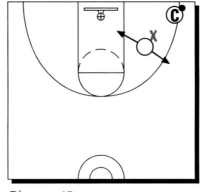

Diagram 45

- In order to keep the box from getting bigger, the defense must be able to deny the ball coming out of the box.

- By using his hand and arm in the passing lane, swiveling his head on back cuts, the defender doesn't allow the ball to be caught by the offense.

- The coach can make the defender more successful at first by limiting the area that the offense can move to get open.

POST DEFENSE—FRONT

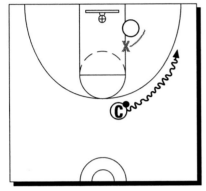

Diagram 46

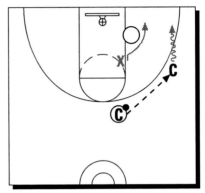

Diagram 47

- The coach starts with the ball at the top of the key while the defender is on the line, up the line against an offensive player in the low post.

- The ball can either be dribbled (Diagram 46) or passed (Diagram 47) to the wing. When that happens, the defender is over the high side of the low post player.

- If the coach on the wing takes a dribble to the baseline to improve his passing angle, the defender steps across in front of the post with his back foot to a full fronting position. The defender gets into a low athletic position and gets his rear into the offensive player's legs.

POST DEFENSE—3-STEP

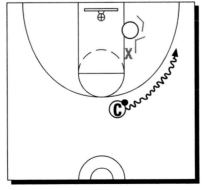

Diagram 48

- This drill calls for a continuation of the defender stepping over the low post to front. As the ball gets to the wing with either a pass or a dribble, the defender uses the same technique to get his feet in front.

- In addition, the coach takes the ball a little lower toward the baseline, and as he does so, the defender goes from the full front position to a denial position on the baseline side by stepping through with his top foot, briefly having the post on his back.

POST DEFENSE—TREE TRUNK

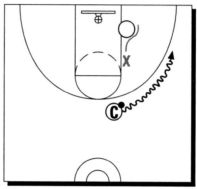

Diagram 49

- The coach starts with the ball on the top of the key and dribbles it to the wing.

- The defender starts in a high-side denial position, and as the ball is dribbled down to the wing area, he slides all the way around the post player, as if he were sliding around a tree, ending up on the baseline side without ever turning his back to the offensive post.

POST DEFENSE—4-POST

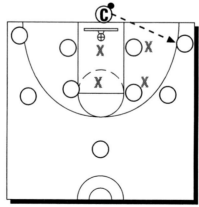

Diagram 50

- Five offensive players remain stationary and pass the ball around the perimeter on the coach's command. Four stationary post players stand at both high post and both low post areas. Each of the four defenders checks one of the post players, working on the correct fronting or pistols position as the ball gets passed around the perimeter.

- The coach should rotate the post defenders so they defend both high and low post areas.

POST DEFENSE—BULL IN THE RING

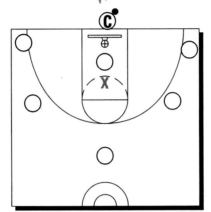

Diagram 51

- The coach starts with the ball on the baseline. Offensive players are stationed in both corners, both wings and the point. The offensive post man and the defender start in the key.

- The coach throws the ball out to one of the perimeter players to begin the action. The post player tries to get open and catch the ball with at least one foot in the key, while the defender tries to deny him the ball. Perimeter players must hold the ball for at least a two-count before passing.

- The drill continues for either a specified amount of time or a specified number of passes.

POST DEFENSE—COVER DOWN

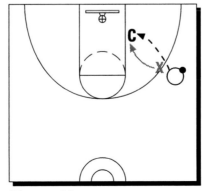

Diagram 52

- The offense begins with the ball on the wing being checked by the defender.

- As the ball gets passed to the coach in the low post, the defender throws his head and steps with his baseline foot first, while sprinting to the low post.

- He stays low and takes away any dribble or middle turn the post player may make. He cannot let the post man split him.

POST DEFENSE—COVER DOWN AND RECOVER

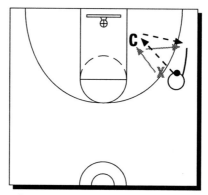

Diagram 53

- This drill adds on to the technique learned in the previous drill.

- After the defender has covered down on the post correctly, the post man can pass the ball back out to the offensive player on the perimeter; at that point, the defender must close out to stop an uncontested shot while influencing any drive to the baseline.

POST DEFENSE—COVER ACROSS

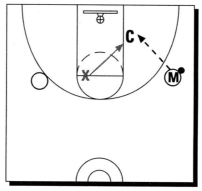

Diagram 54

- A manager starts with the ball on the wing and feeds the ball to the coach in the low post.

- The defender comes from the help-side pistols position and sprints to help in the low post while the ball is in the air.

- At the post, he stays low and takes away any dribble or middle turn the post man may make. He never lets the post split him to the basket.

POST DEFENSE—COVER ACROSS AND RECOVER

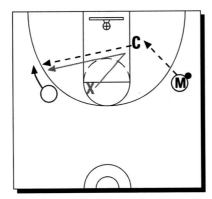

Diagram 55

- This drill is an addition to the previous drill.

- After the defender has correctly covered across on the post, the post kicks the ball out to the help-side perimeter player ,and the defender must recover back and close out to prevent an uncontested shot and influence any drive to the baseline.

FULL-COURT

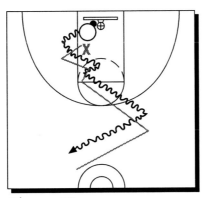

Diagram 56

- In the backcourt, the defender tries to turn the offensive player at least three times, forcing him to change direction.

- Once the dribbler gets to mid-court, the defender tries to keep the dribbler on one side of the floor.

- The defender must keep the offensive player from scoring and also rebound any miss.

FLICK

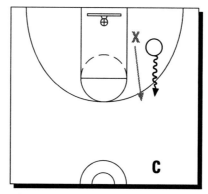

Diagram 57

- The offensive player begins with a slight head start and takes off on a hard dribble.

- The defender chases down the dribbler and flicks the ball ahead to the coach using his inside hand.

- If he successfully flicks the ball to the coach, he immediately changes direction and sprints to the goal, receiving a pass from the coach for a lay-in.

2-ON-1 STOP THE BREAK

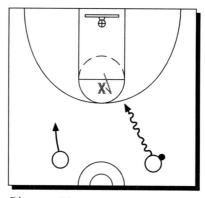

Diagram 58

- The two offensive players start at half court and attack the defender waiting near the foul line.

- The defender uses a jab step to bluff at the dribbler and then drops off, forcing the offense to pick up the ball.

- The goal of the defender is to slow the offense down and not give up a lay-in.

DEFENDING SCREENS—AWAY PERIMETER

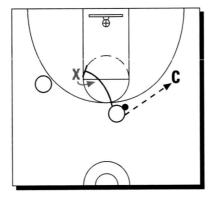

Diagram 59

- The ball starts with an unguarded player at the point who passes to the coach and then goes to set a screen on the defender.

- The defender meets the screen with his inside hand and arm, not letting the screener get contact with his body.

- He then steps over the screener, leading with his inside foot and leg. We go over the top on the perimeter. You should run this drill in a variety of locations.

DEFENDING SCREENS—AWAY POST

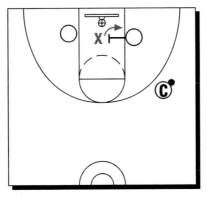

Diagram 60

- The coach starts with the ball on the wing, and when he slaps the ball, an unguarded player in the low post sets a screen on the defender across the key.

- The defender anticipates the screen and meets it with his inside hand and arm, never letting the screener get contact with his body.

- He then steps below the screen with his inside leg. We go below screens in the post area.

DEFENDING SCREENS—DOWN SCREEN

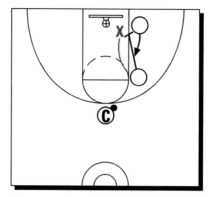

Diagram 61

- The coach begins with the ball on the point. On the slap of the ball, an unguarded player starts on the elbow and goes down the side of the lane to screen the defender.

- The defender meets the screener with his top arm shielding him from contacting his body. He steps under the screen with his top leg and beats the cutter to the spot as he comes off the screen.

DEFENDING SCREENS—PICK-AND-ROLL OVER THE TOP

Diagram 62

- This drill can be done anywhere on the court. An unguarded offensive player sets a ball on the defender.

- The player with the ball tries to use the screen and beat the defender off the dribble.

- X1 keeps his hands to feel the screen. He then crowds the ball handler and gets his lead leg and hips over the top of the screener's feet, forcing the dribbler to widen as he goes off the screen. We call this "skinny up" and get over the screen, and we defend the screen this way against a good perimeter shooter.

DEFENDING SCREENS—PICK-AND-ROLL 3RD MAN

Diagram 63

- This drill uses the same setup as the previous drill. In this drill, as X1 approaches the screener, he steps below the screen with his lead leg. He slides under the screen, not getting caught up in any contact and meeting the dribble on the other side before he can turn the corner.

- We would use this technique against a non-shooter.

DEFENDING SCREENS—PICK-AND-ROLL DOUBLE-TEAM

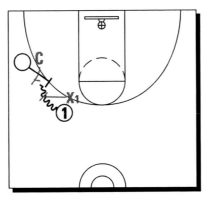

Diagram 64

- The setup for this drill is the same as for the other screen-and-roll drills, except the coach is guarding the screener.

- As the screener approaches the screen, the coach jumps out into the path of the dribbler and X1 stays with the dribbler to form a double team. The two defenders cannot allow the dribbler either to split them or reverse his direction.

DEFENDING SCREENS—DOUBLE-SCREEN

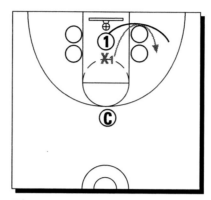

Diagram 65

- O1 and X1 line up in the key, and the coach has the ball at the top of the key to begin the drill. O1 can cut under with a double screen to the perimeter.

- X1 stays right on O1's tail, following him as closely as possible off the double and enabling himself not to be screened.

CONDITIONING—SPRINT—SLIDE CUTOFF

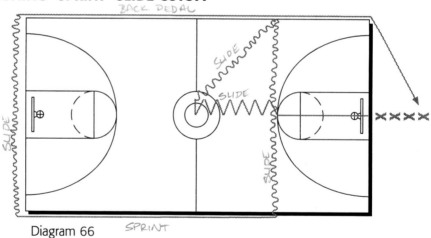

Diagram 66

- Players sprint to the top of the key while communicating with the players crossing the court in front of them.

- When they get to the top of the key, they advance slide to half court.

- At half court they swing step and slide to the hash mark on the sideline and then slide directly across the court, communicating with the players sprinting up behind them.

- Once they get to the sideline, they sprint to the opposite baseline.

- When they arrive there, they slide across the baseline to the opposite corner.

- Next, they sprint back to the end of the court where they started and get back in line.

- While waiting in line, each player stays in a good defensive stance.

- As soon as the player in front of you gets to the top of the key, the next player starts his sprint.

REBOUNDING AWAY FROM THE BALL

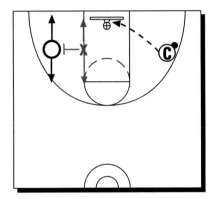

Diagram 67

- The offensive player moves up and down outside the key away from the coach, who has the ball on the opposite wing.

- The defender stays on the line and up the line in the pistols position.

- When the coach shoots, the defender must go out and physically block out the offensive player and secure the rebound.

JAM THE REBOUNDER

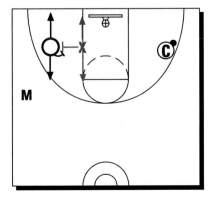

Diagram 68

- This drill is the same as the previous one, except it utilizes an additional skill (described in step 2).

- After the defender rebounds the ball, he looks to outlet the ball to a coach or a manager on the opposite wing, while the offensive player crowds him in an attempt to force him inside and slow down the outlet pass.

1-ON-1 DEFENSIVE DRILL CHART

The following chart is used to keep track of exactly how much time we spend on each phase of the individual one-on-one defense. This chart is helpful not only in planning practice, but also in making sure that we don't neglect certain techniques.

We have found that we are generally very good at points we tend to work on or emphasize the most often, and usually much less consistent in areas we neglect to focus on for any length of time. The chart allows us, on a weekly basis, to tally up the total time we have spent on all phases of one-on-one defense.

If you and your staff are willing to examine videotape of your games and evaluate each player defensively, you will discover that certain tendencies will consistently show up. There will be certain defensive techniques with which your players are strong, regardless of who they are playing, and certain areas where breakdowns consistently occur. You will discover both team tendencies (certain skills that have not been taught well to the whole group) and individual tendencies (certain players who keep failing in the same areas). This process allows you to identify the specific skills that call for more focus for the whole team. It also identifies the individual players who need extra instruction in specific one-on-one defensive skills.

The end result should be better-prepared individuals and a better-prepared team for any and all of our opponents. The coach's job is to give his players a chance to be successful both individually and collectively, regardless of who they are competing against. We should never be out-prepared.

Every coach should create his own time and drill charts and use them to help improve his team's overall defensive skills. I think each coach will be extremely happy with the results.

Additional drill charts will be provided at the end of each chapter for the particular drills that are covered.

1-ON-1 DRILLS	MON TIME	TUE TIME	WED TIME	THR TIME	FRI TIME	SAT TIME
Stance						
Wall						
Step						
Swing Step						
Wave						
Advance-Retreat						
Mirror						
Z Drill						
Ready-Point-Stick						
Force Baseline and Cut Off						
1-on-1 Influence to Side						
Influence Drive						
Approach						
Close Out on Shooter						
Close Out Shoot or Drive						
Close Out off Skip Pass						
Close Out over Screen						
Vision Drill #1						
Vision Drill #2						
Vision Drill #3						
Sprint to Help						
Deny Flash High						
Deny Flash Low						
Deny Flash and Recover						
Jump to the Ball						
Defend the Give-and-Go						
Give-and-Go Either Way						
Defend Pass and Clear Out						
Give-and-Go + Flash						
Give-and-Go Skip and Close Out						
Push the Wing						
Backdoor						
Push the Wing—Influence						

1-ON-1 DRILLS	MON TIME	TUE TIME	WED TIME	THR TIME	FRI TIME	SAT TIME
Point Denial						
Denials out of the Box						
Post Def—Front						
Post Def—3-Step						
Post Def—Tree Trunk						
4-Post						
Bull in the Ring						
Post Cover Down						
Cover Down and Recover						
Post Cover Across						
Cover Across and Recover						
1-on-1 Full Court						
Flick						
2-on-1 Stop the Break						
Screen Away—Perimeter						
Screen Away—Post						
Down Screen						
Ball Screen—Over the Top						
Ball Screen—Third Man						
Ball Screen—Double Team						
Defend Double Screen						
Conditioning—Sprint, Glide, Cut Off						
Rebound away from the Ball						
Jam the Rebounder						

4

Two-on-Two Defensive Drills

SPRINT TO HELP

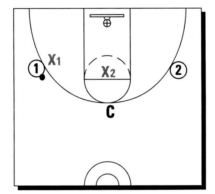

Diagram 69

- In Diagram 69, the drill begins with X1 on the left wing, defending the ball and working on a stance that influences the dribbler to the baseline.

- Defender X2 is off the ball in a pistols position, close enough to put one foot in the box, while at the same time being up the line and on the line.

Diagram 70

- In Diagram 70, the ball is passed to the coach at the top of the key, and both defenders jump to an up-the-line, on-the-line denial position.

TWO ON TWO SPRINT TO HELP (CONT.)

Diagram 71

- In Diagram 71, the ball is passed from the coach to the right wing.

- Immediately, X2 closes out and assumes the responsibilities of the on-the-ball defender, and X1 sprints to help on the line, up the line, close enough to put one foot in the box.

- Keep reversing the ball through the coach at a measured pace in order to teach the footwork and effort necessary to get to the proper sprint-to-help position.

JUMP TO THE BALL

Diagram 72

- This drill should be practiced in different areas on the court each time.

- O1 begins with the ball and passes it to O2 on the wing. As the ball is in the air, X1 jumps in the direction of the ball, getting on the line and up the line.

- The defenders allow the ball to be caught and continue to jump to the ball as it is passed back and forth.

HELP AND RECOVER—GUARD TO GUARD

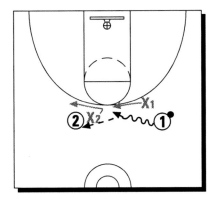

Diagram 73

- O1 dribbles the ball into the gap between X1 and X2. X2 must come from his on-the-line, up-the-line position to stop the ball and then recover back to O2, who has received the pass from O1, who passed the ball when he was stopped.

- This drill continues with O2 driving the gap next and X1 stopping the ball and recovering to an on-the-ball position on O1.

- The defender checking the dribbler works on his footwork to cut off the dribbler by himself.

HELP AND RECOVER—GUARD TO FORWARD

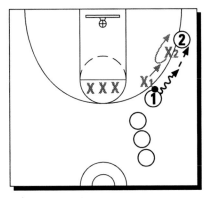

Diagram 74

- This drill is exactly the same as the previous drill, except a guard is working with a player in the forward position, defending the wing.

HELP AND RECOVER—GUARD TO CENTER

Diagram 75

- The ball is penetrated from the point toward the post area by O1.

- X2, who is defending O2 in the post, comes up to bluff at the dribbler to make him stop and then recovers to his post man in a denial position.

- The drill continues as the post (O2) dribbles the ball toward the center, while X1 helps and then recovers to close out on O1.

HELP AND RECOVER—FORWARD TO POST

Diagram 76

- O1 begins with the ball on the wing and is influenced by X1 to dribble baseline toward the post area.

- X2 comes off his man to help stop the ball and then recovers back to the post.

- The drill continues with X1 helping to stop O2, who is dribbling at the post, and then recovering back to O1 as the ball is passed out.

PUSH TO THE WING AND THEN HELP AND RECOVER—FORWARD AND CENTER

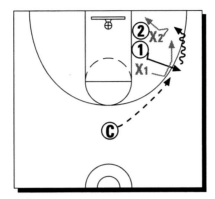

Diagram 77

- This is the same drill as the previously described drill, except for the addition of the coach with the ball on the top of the key and X1 pushing O1 to the wing to catch the ball before he drives.

- Including multiple skills into the same drill needs to be done at a speed at which the athletes can successfully accomplish the goal of the drill.

DEFEND THE BACK SCREEN—NO SWITCH

Diagram 78

- O2 steps up to set a back screen on X1 as O1 passes the ball back to the coach.

- X2 stays off his man in line with the ball, loudly warns X1 of the potential back screen and allows room for X1 to get through and stay with O1.

- X1 explodes in the direction of the ball as the pass is made to the coach, closes to the cutter and puts his head on a swivel sliding over the top of the screen.

DEFEND THE BACK SCREEN BY SWITCHING

Diagram 79

- Same set up to begin this drill, but as O2 steps up to set a back screen, X2 warns X1 about the screen and then calls "switch."

- X2 steps into the path of the cutter (O1) and slides down in position to deny the pass.

- X1 hears the "switch" call and feels behind him for the screener. He then takes his baseline foot and steps over the screener, leaving him in a denial position on X2.

COVER ACROSS

Diagram 80

- The coach enters the ball to O2 at the post. X2 must shut off the baseline drive and make the post turn to the middle.

- X1, who is on the line, up the line from the coach, dives into the post area, taking away any move to the middle by O2. When O2 is stopped, he kicks the ball out to O1, and X1 recovers to close out.

DEFENDING THE BALL SCREEN—OVER THE TOP

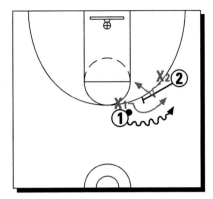

Diagram 81

- Practice this drill in a variety of places on the court. O2 sets a ball screen for O1, and O1 tries to use the screen to beat X1 on the dribble.

- X2 calls out the screen early and then steps out and hedges to make the dribbler widen his path around the screen, thus creating more room for X1.

- X1 hears the screen call and feels for the screener with his hands. He then crowds the dribbler, not allowing him to come off tight on the screen.

- X1 gets his lead leg and shoulder over the screener, lifts his tail end up and slides over the top of the screen.

BALL SCREEN—THIRD MAN

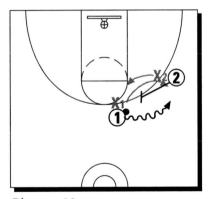

Diagram 82

- Begin this drill the same as in the previous drill. The difference is that instead of going over the top, X1 approaches the screen and then slides below the screener with his lead leg and shoulder and meets the dribbler on the other side.

BALL SCREEN—SWITCH

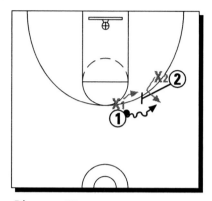

Diagram 83

- As O2 sets the ball screen on X1, X2 calls "screen, switch." X1 then uses the same technique he used to go under the screen (Diagram 82) and then defends O2 so he cannot roll to the basket.

- X2, after calling "screen and switch," steps out and picks up O1 dribbling off the screen.

BALL SCREEN—SWITCH

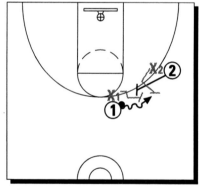

Diagram 84

- O1 again tries to use the screen to beat X1 off the dribble.

- X1 uses the correct technique to go over the top of the screen and traps with X2.

- X1 is responsible for not letting O1 turn back, and X2 is responsible for jumping out and stopping any further penetration in the direction O1 is dribbling.

DEFEND THE CALIFORNIA SCREEN

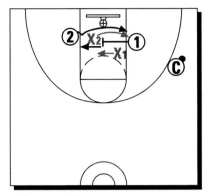

Diagram 85

Diagram 86

- The coach starts with the ball on the wing. On his signal, O1 goes across the key and sets a screen on X2.

- As in the one-on-one drills, X2 always goes under the screener and takes whichever offensive player is the lower man.

- X1 plays the screener on the high side and takes the high cut.

- In diagram 85, O2 cuts low off the screen, and X2 takes him; X1 establishes a pistols position as he continues to guard O1.

- In Diagram 86, O2 uses the screen to cut over the top, and the screener clears out to the opposite side.

- X2 takes the lower offensive player (O1), while X1 takes the high cut and denies the ball to O2, who is coming over the top of the screen.

DEFEND THE HIGH-LOW

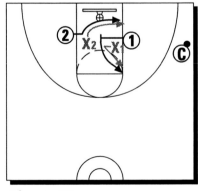

Diagram 87

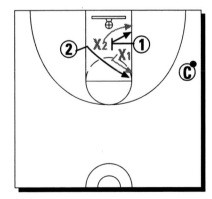

Diagram 88

- The coach has the ball on the wing. On his signal, O1 crosses the key to screen on X2.

- As is taught in the one-on-one drills, X2 always gets below the screener and prepares to take the lower of the two offensive players. He has O2 if he is cutting low off the screen, or O1 if O2 goes over the top and O1 rolls back.

- X1 plays on the screener's high side and takes whichever player takes the higher cut.

- Diagram 87 shows the cutter going under the screen, causing X2 to stay with him and X1 to stay with O1, who is rolling back to the high post.

- Diagram 88 shows the cutter O2 going over the top and being picked up by X1 and the screener rolling back to the low post and being defended by X2 because he is the lower of the two offensive players.

3-ON-2 STOP THE BREAK

Diagram 89

- The top defender, X1, is responsible for stopping the dribbler. For the break to be stopped, he cannot allow penetration past him.

- The back defender, X2, closes out on the player who receives the first pass after the ball has been stopped, and X1 drops to protect the basket area.

- Both defenders only have to stop the quick, easy or unguarded score because, in a real game, the other defenders will arrive within seconds.

FULL COURT

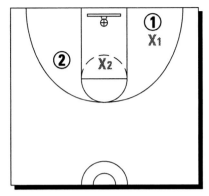

Diagram 90

- Whichever defender is on the ball works on turning the dribbler or forcing him down a sideline, depending on which defense we are working on.

- The off-the-ball defender denies his man the ball while maintaining an on-the-line, up-the-line position.

- If the ball is passed to the other offensive player, the roles switch as he sprints to help.

DEFEND THE BALL-SIDE DOWN SCREEN

Diagram 91

- O1 begins with the ball on the wing and passes to the coach at the top of the circle. O1 then sets a solid down screen on X2.

- X1 jumps to the ball on the pass, and, while sliding down with O1, he moves further from O1 to give X2 room to come between him and the screener.

- X2 slides on the ball side of the down screen, third man, trying to avoid contact.

DEFEND THE DOWN SCREEN AWAY FROM THE BALL

Diagram 92

- A manager passes the ball from the point to the opposite wing as O1 screens down on X2.

- As the pass is made, X1 sprints to help, creating space and enabling X2 to maintain an on-the-line, up-the-line position as he goes through the potential screen, third man.

REBOUND AWAY FROM THE BALL

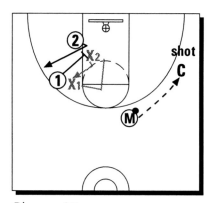

Diagram 93

- This is an addition to the previous screening drill. The manager passes the ball to the coach on the opposite wing to initiate the drill. X1 and X2 defend the screen using the same technique.

- The coach can shoot and let the defenders block out immediately, or he can wait and let the offensive players screen down again.

- The defenders must keep moving in order to be in the correct position and go get their block-out assignments while on the move.

2-ON-2 DRILLS	MON TIME	TUE TIME	WED TIME	THR TIME	FRI TIME	SAT TIME
Sprint to Help						
Jump to the Ball						
Help and Rec. G to G						
Help and Rec. G to F						
Help and Rec. F to C + Push to the Wing						
Back Screen – Switch						
Back Screen – No Switch						
Cover Across						
Ball Screen – Over the Top						
Ball Screen – Third Man						
Ball Screen – Switch						
Ball Screen – Double Team						
California Screen						
Defend High Low						
Screen Across + High Low						
3 on 2 Stop the Break						
2 on 2 Full Court						
Down Screen – Ball Side						
Down Screen – Away						
Rebound Away from the Ball						

5

Three-on-Three Defensive Drills

DEFEND THE SCREEN AWAY—REGULAR

Diagram 94

Diagram 95

- O1 begins with the ball at the top of the circle and passes to either wing and then screens the opposite wing defender.

- The wing who receives the ball squares up and carries the threat of a drive, while the wing who is receiving the screen sets up his man with a V cut so he can cut to the ball or the basket.

- The two wing defenders begin on the line, up the line. The defender on the side where the ball is entered must readjust his position to influence the receiver while the ball is in the air, so that by the time it is caught, he is in the correct position.

- The defender on the opposite wing must sprint to help, making himself difficult to screen by not letting the screener get to his body.

- He then slips under the screen and prepares to meet the cutter, whichever way he uses the screen.

- X1, the ball defender, jumps in the direction of the pass and then hedges out to help X3 through the screen. X1 stays high and gives space while he adjusts his position so he can be on the line, up the line with vision of the ball.

- Diagram 95 shows how the drill can continue so that all defenders are practicing each of the techniques.

DEFEND THE SCREEN AWAY—SWITCH

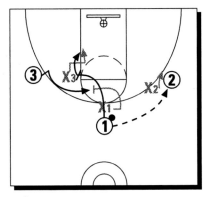

Diagram 96

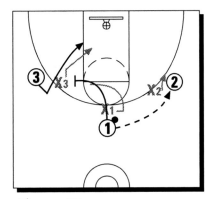

Diagram 97

- O1 initiates the drill from the top of the circle by passing to either wing and screening opposite. The other offensive players follow the same procedure as in the previous drill.

- The defenders away from the pass are going to make a predetermined switch based on which offensive player cuts high and which cuts low.

- In this case, X3 goes below the screen and takes away the roll to the basket by O1 or the back cut by O3, and X1 takes whichever man cuts high.

- In Diagram 97, O3 uses the screen to back cut, so X3 stays with him, and X1 stays with X1, since he is the man who stays high.

BALL SCREEN—OVER THE TOP

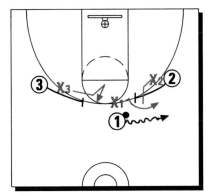

Diagram 98

- This drill can and should be run in a variety of places on the floor. In Diagram 98, O1 starts with the ball on the top of the key, with O2 and O3 on each wing.

- Both offensive players on the wings come up and set a ball screen for O1, who can go in either direction off a screen.

- The defenders involved in the ball screen (X1 and X2) us the same techniques that they practiced in the two-on-two drill to get over the top of the screen.

- The third defender, X3, comes off his man in a position to help on any roll to the basket and then recovers to check O3 in an on-the-line, up-the-line position.

BALL SCREEN—THIRD MAN, SWITCH AND DOUBLE TEAM

Each of these methods of defending the screen on the ball can be done using the same techniques as the two-on-two drills, plus adding a third offensive and defensive player as shown in the previous drill. Both offensive players establish a screening position on either side of the ball, and the dribbler can choose the side he wants to go to with the defenders either going (a) third man, (b) switching, or (c) double-teaming. The defender not involved in the ball screen comes off and helps on any of the offensive players slipping to the basket and then recovers back to his assignment.

DEFEND THE GIVE-AND-GO

Diagram 99

- O1 begins with the ball and passes to either O2 or O3 and makes a hard basket cut.

- X1 jumps in the direction of the pass, snaps his head on a swivel and stays with the cutter down the key, staying on the ball side.

- X3 sprints to help and denies the point reversal or back cut by O3.

CONTINUATION OF DEFENDING THE GIVE-AND-GO

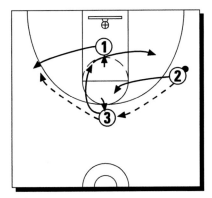

Diagram 100

- In order for the above drill to have continuity, the defenders can work on the correct positioning without intercepting any of the passes.

- To continue the drill, O1 fills the opposite wing after making a give-and-go cut, and the wing player opposite the first pass fills the point to receive a pass and swing the ball. This movement will give each player multiple repetitions at defending the give-and-go from each place in the drill.

HELP AND RECOVER

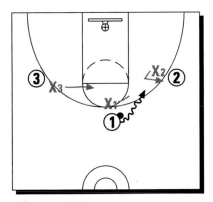

Diagram 101

- O1 begins with the ball and with offensive teammates on either side of him.

- He drives the ball into either gap. The defender on the ball works to stop the dribbler by himself, but his teammate must be ready to help by stopping the ball and recovering back to the correct position on his man.

- The offside defender (X3) must stay in a position to prevent the skip pass and still be in a position to help.

HELP AND RECOVER FROM THE WING

Diagram 102

- This drill is the same as the previous drill, except that it is done from the side of the court which changes the box.

- The third defender must identify how far off to come help keep the ball in the box without letting his man slip to the basket.

DEFEND TO SMASH

Diagram 103

- The smash (or high post rub) is often used as the entry cut on set offenses.

- O1 enters the ball to O2 on the wing and makes a hard basket cut off high post player O3.

- X1 must jump to the ball and go ball side of the high post screen. X2 pressures the wing. X3 verbally warns X1 and then hedges out into the path of the cutter, forcing him to widen and allowing X1 to get through. This position also allows X3 to deny the ball to the high post once the cutter has passed.

3-ON-3 PLUS 1—COVER ACROSS AND RECOVER

Diagram 104

- O1 enters the ball on the wing to O2, who passes the ball into an unguarded post player. O4 holds the ball until the rotation has taken place and then passes it back out to the perimeter.

- X1 jumps to the ball, and X2 adjusts to pressure the ball.

- X3 sprints across as the ball is entered to the post and then closes out on O3 on the kick-out pass.

COVER ACROSS AND BLOCK OUT

Diagram 105

- This drill is an addition to the previous drill.

- All defensive responsibilities remain the same as the ball is swung and entered into the post.

- When the ball gets passed out of the post, O3 shoots. X2 and X3 use the away-from-the-ball block-out techniques. X3 closes out on O3, contests the shot and then blocks out the shooter.

3-ON-3 PLUS 1—LIVE TO SCORE

Diagram 106

- This drill uses the same principles as the three-on-three cover across, except the offense attempts to score from the perimeter or the post positions.

- O4 can move to either side of the key. The perimeter players must stay stationary, but can score on a kick-out and can feed the post when he is on their side of the floor. The defenders have to really work to continually cover across on the post and still recover to their man.

DEFENSIVE GAME

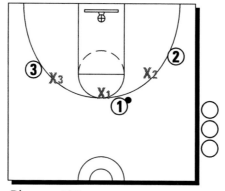

Diagram 107

- This is a live game for both teams, but you can only score on defense. Additional teams are waiting to play the winning team.

- The defensive team gets one point for a stop and an additional point for a charge. If the offense scores, the offensive players get to go on defense.

- First team to score four points wins and gets to start on defense against the new team.

THREE STOPS

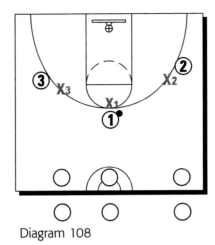

Diagram 108

- This drill challenges the defensive team to get three consecutive stops before it is finished. Other three-man teams waiting at half court come at the defensive team in waves, attempting to score. As soon as your team either gets stopped or scores, the players go quickly to the sidelines, and the next team immediately attacks the defensive team from half court.

- Any score or foul against the defense puts the number of stops back at zero.

DEFENDING THE FLEX

Diagram 109

- The *flex offense* presents some unique challenges to a defensive team because of the type and number of consecutive screens involved in the pattern. By itself, each cut and screen is not that difficult to defend, but when they are sequenced together, it can provide problems for your defense. It is time well spent to practice defending the specific screens that you will see from a team that runs this offense.

- If your defenders understand the type and location of the screens, they can anticipate and successfully defend each one. Players need to know how to defend all three spots.

- To begin the drill, two coaches position themselves on the elbow opposite the players. One coach has a ball and will pass to the player coming off the back screen; the other coach will receive a pass from O3 and then pass to the player coming off the down screen.

- The pattern for the offense is as follows: O3 starts with a ball and initiates the drill by passing across to the coach, who is going to make a return pass to O2 coming up off the down screen; O1 cuts off a back screen by O2, a move that is immediately followed by O3 setting a down screen for O2 and then opening to the ball.

- X1 must jump to the ball as O3 passes to the coach; he should then go over the top of O2's screen, going third man and denying the pass from the coach.

- X2 starts on the baseline side of the post and must get around basket side of O2 and get off the ball so X1 can go third man over the screen. X2 must then jump to the ball so he can go third man through the down screen set by O3 and deny the pass from the coach.

- X3 starts on the ball and jumps in the direction of the pass when O3 passes to the coach. He then drops on the ball side with O3 and stays off to the ball so that X2 can go third man, keeping aware of O3 opening up to the ball after the screen.

- Coaches should teach the offensive pattern first, and then one screen at a time, until the players are ready to put the whole sequence together.

DEFENDING FLEX BY SWITCHING

Diagram 110

Diagram 111

- This strategy is another option for your defense when defending the flex offense.

- The offensive players run the same pattern as in the previous drill.

- Diagram 110 shows the initial positions of the offensive and defensive players. Diagram 111 shows where the players are after switching the screens.

FULL COURT

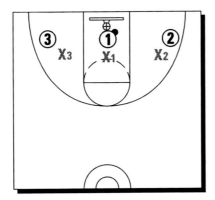

Diagram 112

- The defender on the ball works on turning the dribbler or forcing him down the sideline, depending on which team defense is being worked on.

- The other two defenders deny their man the ball while maintaining an on-the-line, up-the-line position.

- This drill can consist of one direction and stop, or the teams can play to a specific score; the winning team stays.

3-ON-2 PLUS 1 FULL-COURT STOP THE BREAK

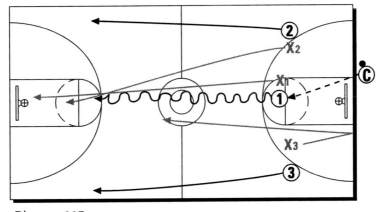

Diagram 113

- The three offensive players and the three defensive players all begin on the backcourt, foul line extended.

- The coach stands on the end line and calls the name of a defender while he throws the ball in to one of the offensive players. The defensive player whose name was called has to touch the baseline before he can sprint back on defense. The offense can go down court three-on-two as soon as it receives the ball.

- The two defenders play the break the same as they did in the three-on-two drill, except this time a third defender is hustling to get back, so they only have to hold off the offense for a couple of seconds. The defenders must communicate to match up as the third defender hopefully gets back in time to make it a three-on-three situation.

3-ON-3 DEFENSIVE DRILL CHART

3-ON-3 DRILLS	MON TIME	TUE TIME	WED TIME	THR TIME	FRI TIME	SAT TIME
Screen Away – Regular						
Screen Away – Switch						
Ball Screen – Over the Top + Help						
Ball Screen – Either Way						
Ball Screen – Switch and Double Team						
Defend Give and Go						
Help and Recover						
Smash						
3 on 3 + 1 Cover Down						
3 on 3 + 1 Cover Down + Shot and Blockout						
3 on 3 + 1 Live to Score						
Defensive Game						
3 Stops						
Flex						
3 on 2 + 1 Full						
3 on 3 Full						

6

Four-on-Four Defensive Drills

SHELL—POSITION

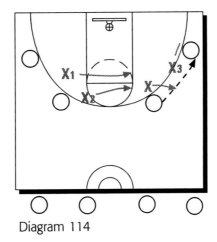

Diagram 114

- Four offensive players evenly space themselves around the three-point line.

- The ball is passed around the horn on a coach's signal, with each offensive player holding the ball for about two seconds.

- As the ball is passed and held, the coach checks and makes corrections on the foot and hand position of each player. Players move while the ball is in the air and allow the ball to be passed through them, even when they are in a denial position. After the drill has been successfully completed, the next four players come in on offense and the offense moves quickly to defense.

SHELL + EXCHANGE

Diagram 115

- Players use the same setup and rotation as in the previous drill.

- This time, as the ball reverses sides, the two players away from the ball side exchange positions.

- The two defenders move with the offensive players, going third man, keeping vision, and an on-the-line, up-the-line position.

SHELL + DOWN SCREEN

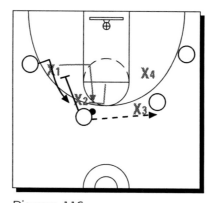

Diagram 116

- From the shell setup, the top offensive player away from the ball sets a down screen on the lower defender when the ball is reversed.

- The two defenders communicate the screen, go third man and stay in the correct position.

- In all the shell drills, it is better to have one coach watching each side of the court.

SHELL + EXCHANGE AND CALIFORNIA SCREEN

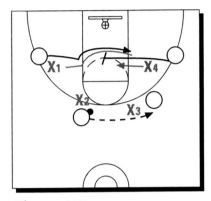

Diagram 117

- The players use the same shell setup as in the previous drill, but when the coach calls "exchange," the players away from the ball exchange top to bottom.

- When the coach calls "screen," the lower player on the ball side screens across the key.

- Defenders play the exchange and the California screen as previously described.

SHELL + ROTATION

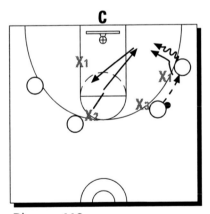

Diagram 118

- This drill is the same as the previous drill, except that as the ball gets passed to either lower offensive player, the coach can give a signal for them to drive on the defender.

- We like to give a silent signal (fist) so that the defense is not warned and has to react instinctively. Defensively, we rotate our guard down to help stop the baseline drive, and as the ball gets passed back out, we return to an on-the-line, up-the-line position.

SHELL + 2 ROTATION TO STOP THE DRIVE

Diagram 119

- This calls for the same four-on-four shell setup as in the previous drill, but with two additional unguarded players in the corners.

- Anytime the ball is passed to the corner players, they drive hard to the basket until they are stopped by the proper defensive rotation.

4-ON-4 + POST COVER DOWN

Diagram 120

- This is the same shell drill as the others, except it calls for the addition of an unguarded post player.

- We can work on cover down or cover across every time the ball is entered into the post.

- The emphasis is on correct position and quick reaction to a post pass.

4-ON-4 PLUS POST LIVE TO SCORE

Diagram 121

- This drill is the same as the previous drill, except the offense is allowed to attempt to score either from a post feed or a kick-out to the perimeter players.

- This drill is the best help-and-recover drill we have found.

- The defensive players stay on until they have recorded a total of five stops.

4-ON-4-ON 4—3 STOPS

Diagram 122

- The four defensive players try to make three consecutive stops on alternating offensive teams.

- The offensive teams have no restrictions, and as soon as one team has either been stopped or scores, the next team comes on the attack.

- A foul by the defense counts as a score for the offense.

- This drill is a competitive one that requires a quick transition to the next team coming in from half court.

4-ON-3 + TRAIL DEFENDER

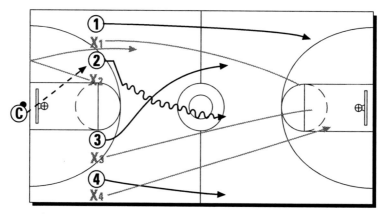

Diagram 123

- Four offensive and four defensive players start in backcourt across the foul line extended. The coach calls one of the defender's names as he throws the ball to the offense. That defender must touch the baseline before he retreats to help.

- The other three defenders dive to the key, stop the ball and keep the offense from getting an easy shot until the fourth defender gets back and they can match up.

4-ON-4 ANTI-REVERSAL

Diagram 124

- O1 enters the ball to O2 on the wing against X2's pressure. X1 jumps to the ball, going on the ball side of the high post screen.

- X3 goes under the high post man and off to the ball, allowing X1 to get over the screen, while X3 is in position to deny the reversal through the high post.

- X4 sprints to help and is in position not only to help on the smash cut, but also to deny reversal to O4.

4-ON-4 FULL COURT

Diagram 125

- The defender on the ball works to either turn the dribbler or force him to a side, depending on what the team emphasis is.

- The defenders off the ball deny their man the ball while maintaining an on-the-line, up-the-line position.

4-ON-4 DRILLS	MON TIME	TUE TIME	WED TIME	THR TIME	FRI TIME	SAT TIME
Shell Drill – Position						
Shell Drill – Exchange						
Shell Drill – Down Screen						
Shell Drill – California Screen						
Shell Drill – Rotation						
Shell + 2 in the Corners						
Help and Recover						
4 on 4 + 1 Cover Down						
4 on 4 + 1 Live to Score						
4 on 4 Three Stops						
4 on 3 Plus Defensive Trailer						
4 on 4 Anti-Reversal						
4 on 4 Full Court						

7

Five-on-Five Defensive Drills

WALK-THROUGH

Diagram 126

- This drill is used to get players to work on their position and provides them with an opportunity to ask questions if they get into any positions on the floor that they aren't sure how to defend.

- The coach has the ball and calls "move," which means that the five offensive players all are free to move any direction they wish at either a walking or slow-motion pace. They can set screens or use screens.

- When the coach calls "freeze," everyone stops, and the position of the defenders is critiqued. Players can also stop at any time to ask questions about how they should defend certain situations.

MIXER

- The offense can run the five-man motion offense while the defense works on positioning.

- The coach shoots the ball, and all five defenders must block out. The coach can have the defenders play with their hands behind their backs, working only on their feet, until the ball is shot.

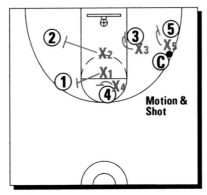

Diagram 127

MIXER AND BREAK

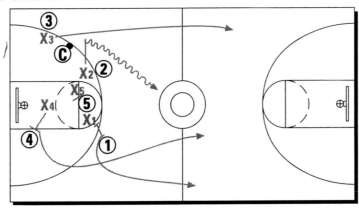

Diagram 128

- This drill is the same as the previous one, except if the defenders block out and complete all their responsibilities, they run their fast-break pattern to the other end.

5-ON-0 FAST BREAK AND DEFENSIVE TRANSITION

- The coach shoots, and the defenders block out and run their fast-break pattern down the floor 5-on-0. Once they score, they immediately dive back to the defensive end, sprinting the middle third of the floor and checking to locate the ball over their inside shoulder.

- The coach at the offensive end inbounds the ball to a coach at half court, who, in turn, passes to the offense, which has waited on this end. The defenders must find their men, get in correct position and stop the ball from penetrating.

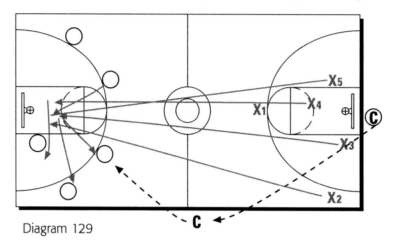

Diagram 129

DEFEND–BREAK–TRANSITION BACK

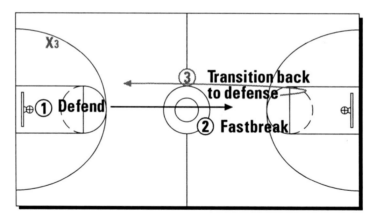

Diagram 130

- This drill is an addition to the previous drill. The defensive players must first get a stop before they can fast break 5-on-0.

- Next, the defense must make a quick defensive dive to stop any easy baskets.

- The defensive players can stay, as long as they get a defensive stop and then a transition stop.

5-MAN RUSH

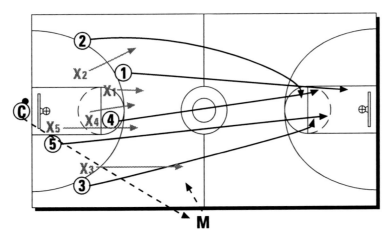

Diagram 131

- The offense runs five-man motion while the defense works on correct positioning.

- The coach throws the ball down the floor to a manager or coach at half court. The defensive team converts to offense and the offensive team converts to defense. The manager can throw the ball to any of the offensive players, while the defense must find and adjust to stop any easy baskets.

CHANGE DRILL

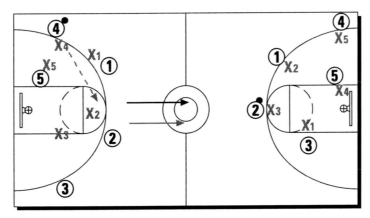

Diagram 132

- This drill is a five-on-five, with the offense running motion and the defense working on positioning.

- The coach calls "change," and the man with the ball hands the ball to the defense. All five offensive players convert to defense while the new offensive team fast breaks.

- When you convert to defense, you cannot guard the man who was guarding you. The focus of this drill is for the players to communicate so that they are checking and finding unguarded players.

SWITCH AND CHANGE

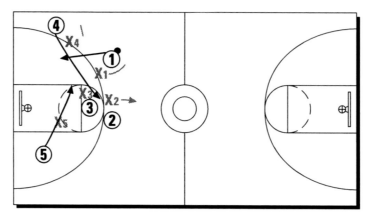

Diagram 133

- This drill is exactly like the previous one, except the coach can call "change" or "switch." When switch is called, the defense becomes the offense at the end where you are playing, and the new defenders must again guard a different player than the player who was guarding them.

- This drill emphasizes communication and recovering to a man.

5-ON-5 DRILLS	MON TIME	TUE TIME	WED TIME	THR TIME	FRI TIME	SAT TIME
Walk Through						
5 on 5 Mixer						
Mixer and Break						
5 on 0 Break + Def. Transition						
Defense – Break – Transition						
Five Man Rush						
Change Drill						
Switch and Change Drill						

Conclusion

In preparing our team on defense, we leave as little as possible to chance. Our players should have confidence that they can defend any situation they encounter. There will be very little that our opponents can do that we have not broken down into drill form and worked on ahead of time.

The time charts have proven especially valuable to our staff because they enable us to keep accurate records of how much time we spend on each particular phase of the defense. Whenever we have had major breakdowns, it is always because we have not dedicated enough time to that particular skill.

The building of pride in your defense begins with the fundamentals done correctly at an individual level (one-on-one) and is gradually extended to include more players until you can defend five-on-five.

An individual player who has to depend on his defensive play to earn a spot on the roster or to get playing time will be someone who must really develop a sense of pride and satisfaction in his technique and effort. Many times, a few players like this can convey that defensive determination to the entire squad.

When the individual members of your team begin to master the defensive skills, the whole team is able to recognize it, and the all-important pride factor develops. When any team reaches this level, we know as coaches that we are well on our way to a successful season.

About the Author

Bob Huggins is the head men's basketball coach at West Virginia University, a position he assumed in 2007. Previously, he served in the same position at Kansas State University during the 2006 season. Before that, he was the head men's basketball coach at the University of Cincinnati from 1989 to 2005. During his 16 years at the helm of the Bearcats' program, Huggins compiled an impressive 399-127 record, making him the winningest coach in U.C. history. In the process, he led his last 14 Cincinnati squads to the NCAA Tournament—the third-longest streak among active coaches in the nation.

During his impressive career, Huggins has been awarded many coaching honors, including the Ray Meyer Award as the Conference USA Coach of the Year in 1997-98, 1998-99, and 1999-2000. He was named co-national coach of the year by The Sporting News in 2004-05 and was also Basketball Times' selection for national coach of the year for the 1997-98 season.

Huggins began his coaching career as a graduate assistant at his alma mater, the University of West Virginia, in 1977. Subsequent coaching stints included Ohio State (1978-80), Walsh College (1980-83), Central Florida (1983), and the University of Akron (1984-89). In his career, Huggins' teams have won 20 or more games in all but four of his 25 campaigns, including 30 or more twice.

Born in Morgantown, West Virginia, Huggins grew up in Gnadenhutten, Ohio, where he played high school basketball for his father, Charles Huggins, at Gnadenhutten Indian Valley South. Bob and his wife, June, have two daughters, Jenna and Jacqueline.